BUSINESS ISSUES, COMPETITION AND ENTREPRENEURSHIP

TAXING A POLLUTING MONOPOLY WITH PRIVATE INFORMATION

BUSINESS ISSUES, COMPETITION AND ENTREPRENEURSHIP

Additional books in this series can be found on Nova's website under the Series tab.

Additional E-books in this series can be found on Nova's website under the E-book tab.

BUSINESS ISSUES, COMPETITION AND ENTREPRENEURSHIP

TAXING A POLLUTING MONOPOLY WITH PRIVATE INFORMATION

MANEL ANTELO
AND
MARIA L. LOUREIRO

NOVINKA

Nova Science Publishers, Inc.
New York

For permission to use material from this book please contact us:
Telephone 631-231-7269; Fax 631-231-8175
Web Site: http://www.novapublishers.com

LIBRARY OF CONGRESS CATALOGING-IN-PUBLICATION DATA

Antelo, Manel.
Taxing a polluting monopoly with private information / Manel Antelo and
Maria L. Loureiro.
p. cm.
Includes index.
ISBN 978-1-61728-954-5 (softcover)
1. Environmental impact charges. 2. Business intelligence. 3.
Monopolies. I. Loureiro, Maria L. II. Title.
HJ5316.A58 2010
336.1'6--dc22-2010026184

Published by Nova Science Publishers, Inc. ✢ New York

CONTENTS

PREFACE

Firms have usually more information about their technology than third parties, and this may be used opportunistically. In this chapter, the authors examine how a regulator can mitigate the potential opportunistic behavior of a polluting monopolist, when imposing environmental taxes in a context of asymmetric information about the firm's production (and emissions) technology. The authors use a two-period model in which the asymmetric information problem is resolved when production and emissions levels of the first period are publicly observed at the beginning of the second period and signaling then holds. In this set up, the authors find that whenever the regulator's environmental conscience is sufficiently high, the monopolist wishes to be perceived as a firm that pollutes a low amount. As a reaction, the regulator better aligns its incentives with those of the polluting firm by charging in the first period–the asymmetric information period–a tax not higher than that imposed, in expected terms, under symmetric information. So, green policies based on time-increasing taxes may be rationalized in a context of asymmetric information when signaling is costly. The authors also show that the presence of asymmetric information and signaling reduce the level of expected social welfare as compared to that in a symmetric information context, and diminishes the amount of under-taxation with respect to marginal damage. The case of a regulator with a low environmental conscience is also examined in this chapter.

Chapter 1

INTRODUCTION

Many activities of production and consumption have significant environmental impacts due to the widespread use of fossil fuels and other environmentally harmful substances. The size of such effects is of concern not only because of their direct impacts on the production and consumption processes, but also due to their effects on third parties not directly involved into the production or consumption of the goods in question (environmental externalities). Economists have paid increasing attention to the question of whether it is possible to use economic instruments to improve the quality of the environment and, in particular, to mitigate the effects of such environmental externalities.

Much of the economic literature on environmental externalities has focussed on how to correct them at the least possible cost. Two economic mechanisms often suggested to correct such externalities are pollution taxes, and standards to control the maximum level of desirable pollution produced by firms. As expected, by charging a polluting agent a given amount for each unit of pollution, the tax gives an incentive to reduce pollution. In contrast, a standard sets up a limit of pollution that cannot be exceeded (Helfand, 1999). Pollution taxes are often referred as having clear efficiency advantages over standards, because firms are free to choose to what extend to abate pollution and how. However, it should be noted that if only one firm or a fixed number of identical firms are being regulated in a world without uncertainty and where perfect information holds, then taxes and standards result in the same level of efficiency.

The superiority of the tax mechanism occurs specially when firms are heterogeneous with respect to costs (Baumol and Oates, 1988). For instance, if firms have different abatement costs, such costs are minimized when marginal costs of abatement are equalized across firms. In this way, those firms for which abatement is not very costly will reduce pollution more than firms whose abatement is expensive. On the opposite, the establishment of a uniform pollution standard requires the same environmental performance of all firms. The case of different firms in technologically terms (different cost realizations of a firm) that operate under asymmetric information is treated in detail in this book chapter.

A pollution tax has also desirable properties in terms of industry structure and performance. Spulber (1985) has shown that for identical firms in a perfectly competitive market, a pollution tax equal to the marginal damage caused by pollution—a Pigouvian tax (Pigou, 1922)— will achieve not only the correct marginal conditions for optimality, but also it will make possible that the optimal number of firms remain in the industry in the long run. Finally, a pollution tax is more effective than standards at encouraging technological innovation to reduce pollution. Milliman and Prince (1989) (for the case of identical firms) and Jung et al. (1996) (for heterogeneous firms) find that pollution taxes lead to greater incentives for technological change.

Direct taxation on pollution and indirect environmental levies have been introduced in many developed countries, indicating a shift in demand for a cleaner environment. Although more recent research indicates that the cost of a cleaner environment may be somewhat higher than previously indicated by the "double-dividend" hypothesis,[1] environment-related taxes are becoming an increasingly important part of the fiscal systems of OECD countries (Morgenstern, 1995). As indicated by OECD data (OECD, 2006), all OECD member countries apply several environmentally related taxes. To illustrate, database operated by OECD and the European Environment Agency currently details about 375 such *taxes* in OECD countries—plus some 250 environmentally related fees and charges. The taxes raise revenues in the order of 2-2.5% of GDP. About 90% of this revenue stems from taxes on motor vehicle fuels and motor vehicles, whereas revenue-raising is not a

[1] The double-dividend approach was reframed by the more recent literature, which emphasizes the fact that environmental taxes may cause potentially significant distortions in the factors and product markets that undermine the double-dividend hypothesis, although virtually *any* environmental regulatory instrument (including taxes, regulations, and tradable emissions permits) tends to compound pre-existing distortions in the tax system—a cost that is recognized as tax interactions or interdependency effects. See Bovenberg (1999), Morgenstern (1996) and Schöb (2003) for discussions on this subject.

prime motivation for many other taxes applied. Figures for other countries show that Norway, the UK and Denmark raise more than the average level of revenue through environment-related taxes (European Commission, 1998; OECD, 2006).

The OECD data also indicate that environmental tax revenues rose during the 1990s, partly because new taxes on waste and energy were introduced in many member countries. For instance, several European countries and Japan introduced tax power generation; Scandinavian countries and the Netherlands levy carbon dioxide taxes; Scandinavian countries, Denmark, Switzerland, France, Italy, the Czech Republic, Spain (region of Galicia), and Korea levy sulphur taxes on oil products and electricity generation; Sweden and France apply a nitrogen oxide tax; Denmark and Norway levy a tax on chlorinated solvents; Italy, the US and the Czech Republic are among countries which tax lubricant oils; Belgium, Canada, Germany and Sweden are among those which tax pesticides; and Sweden and the US tax commercial fertilizers.

The OECD and European Commission data also show remarkable effects linked to the introduction of specific taxes. For example, the tax on plastic bags applied in Ireland since 2002 has contributed to the reduction in their use by more than 90%. Also, the ecological tax reform in Germany has led to a 2-3% reduction in energy consumption and carbon dioxide emissions since 1999.

However, in spite of the broad application of taxation mechanisms, and their previously discussed superiority in terms of efficiency with respect to standards, we should be aware that such positive outlook is the result of some restrictive assumptions in which theoretical models are based. For example, most previous literature considers that an additional unit of pollution from a given source causes the same marginal damage as the unit of pollution from another source; and that marginal benefits of abatement are decreasing, while marginal costs of abatement are increasing. An additional consideration that is most relevant for the present chapter is the assumption that all parties (the regulator setting taxes and polluting firms) share the same information about technology, and resulted levels of emissions. However, this assumption is rather simplistic and in most cases, incorrect. A more realistic set up is the assumption that firms have more information about their production technology and emitted pollution than the regulator, which generates an environment of asymmetric information. Asymmetric information problems have been extensively considered in other topics by Baron and Besanko (1985), and Baron and Myerson (1982), among others. What we examine in this book chapter is the consideration that polluting firms may differ in their production and emissions costs and, consequently, in their levels of production and emissions. That is, in addition to the fact that the regulator ignores the cost of a particular firm, such cost may vary across firms, and as a consequence, the information problem faced by the regulator is magnified. Taxation in the context of asymmetric information with heterogeneous polluting firms is a field in which environmental literature is currently developing, although it is still scarce. To our knowledge, only Antelo and Loureiro (2009) and Benchekroun and Van Long (1998) deal with this issue in the context of duopolistic markets. The goal of this book chapter is to shed light about the role that different informational scenarios play in such tax setting environment.

To this end, the chapter focuses in the case where the policymaker has imperfect information. The source of informational asymmetry by which the polluting firm has more information about its technology and emissions than the regulator here considered—that we refer as *vertical informational asymmetry*—is not only a major difficulty in the policymaking arena. It may also lead firms to have, in a dynamic setting, the potential and the incentive to exploit their informational advantage with the aim of undermining the intended goals of external parties such as the policymaker. After observing a firm's action in a given period (the output it produces in such period for example), the policymaker has the potential to adjust its regulatory action for the next period in order to counteract the firm's strategic behavior. This may produce a conflict between the firms' objective and the social welfare objective of the regulator that may significantly affect the optimal level of pollution taxes.

In this context, it seems appropriate to examine the regulator's behavior in a dynamic context in which polluters act strategically, particularly when polluters have an informational advantage, and they are large enough to have an effect on the market and regulatory actions taken. Furthermore, another aspect treated in the current chapter is the role played by the regulator's environmental conscience or environmental values on tax setting mechanisms. Environmental values are of importance in order to set up environmental policies that may impact the economic growth. In this sense, regulator's actions may be in line with citizen's preferences. A growing body of literature addresses the role of environmental values in terms of countries joining international environmental agreements or fulfilling certain quality standards (Lange, 2006).

To our knowledge, the role of the regulator's environmental values has not been yet covered in relation with the previous taxation literature. In this regard, two specific cases are considered: first, a scenario in which the regulator is quite concerned about internalizing environmental emissions in order to maximize the social welfare function. This scenario corresponds with the establishment of Pigouvian taxes under asymmetric information. In a second scenario, the regulator pursues to maximize the social welfare function with low environmental considerations, aiming to maximize output. In this case, subsidies to output arise as the solution of the social welfare maximization problem. This later case corresponds quite well with current economic conditions, which incline regulators in developed countries to revive their interest in stimulating output production and consumption activities. This scenario is also applicable to the developing world, in which regulators aim to increase social welfare by increasing production and consumption of basic goods, postponing environmental considerations for later stages of development, which may be associated with higher income and welfare per capita. The relationship between per capita income and pollution has been well documented in the literature with the Kutznes growth curve.

Therefore, the aim of this research is to explore the extent to which the existence of private information concerning the technology of polluting firms, and the possibility of disclosing it, as well as the regulator's environmental conscience, affect the optimal level of pollution taxes in a dynamic context. This dynamic setting allows us to understand the strategic interaction of firms and the regulator. In the following model, we consider the case of a single firm (monopoly) that may be a firm that produces and pollutes a large or small amount. That is, based on the existence of uncertainty, the firm may turn out to be productively efficient or not so efficient. In the model, a firm that turns out to be productively efficient, produces a large amount of output at low cost (it is a low-cost firm). Such firm consequently pollutes more than a non productively efficient one, which produces less amount of output, and less pollution (a high-cost firm). The firm and the regulator are engaged in a two-period incomplete information game with the following timing. In period 1, the regulator, without knowledge of the firm's type, announces and commits to a per-unit output (or a per-unit emissions) tax for this period, and the firm then produces an output level which generates a given level of emissions. In period 2, the regulator may use the firm's level of output and emissions to draw conclusions about its type (low-cost or high-cost firm). The regulator then sets a per-unit output tax (or per-unit emissions tax). In our set up, the scenario in which the regulator uses the output and emissions level in period 1 to set the level of taxation in period 2 (the signaling context) is compared with the benchmark case in which the regulator and the firm share the same amount of information (symmetric information context), so the regulator does not require to observe a firm's action of period 1.

If we consider a monopolist whose production damages the environment, two types of distortions exist that affect the social welfare function: the distortion due to the environmental damage (externality caused to third parties), and that of the firm's underproduction linked to the exercise of market power. As a consequence, the regulator, when designing the optimal environmental tax in a symmetric information regime, simply balances the production and the environmental damage. In such a trade off, and although the monopolist's expected output is lower than the socially efficient level, and any output tax reduces its production further, a positive environmental tax is optimal when the policymaker's valuation of the environment is high enough.

Things may change drastically in the presence of asymmetric information and the consequent signaling activity by polluting firm. In this case, when selecting the optimal environmental tax for period 1, we must add a signaling effect to be considered by the regulator. The indirect-signaling effect works as follows: if the regulator's environmental conscience is sufficiently high, a low-cost firm (efficient in productive terms) has an incentive to misrepresent itself as a high-cost firm (inefficient in productive terms), with the aim of paying a lower tax in period 2. This encourages the regulator to commit to a lower tax in period 1 than under symmetric information. In fact, in order to outweigh the incentive for a low-cost polluting firm to misrepresent itself as high-cost, the regulator has to make the downward output and emissions distortions of period 1 more costly, which is achieved by reducing the imposed tax. On the other hand, the direct-signaling effect induces the firm to produce and pollute in period 1 less than under symmetric information. This effect also encourages the regulator to reduce taxes in the signaling context. Thus, taxes change while the information evolves from incomplete to complete.

In the following sections the two-period environmental tax game is examined to find the separating sequential equilibrium. In such equilibrium it is shown that to convince the regulator that the firm is of a high-cost type, the high-cost polluter needs to distort its period 1 output below the level corresponding to symmetric information. As a result, signaling significantly leads the optimal period 1 to be not greater than that relative to the symmetric information setting. Hence, while the imposed tax, in expected terms, is constant across periods under symmetric information, this no longer holds in the context of asymmetric information. In this case, a non-decreasing time pattern on taxes emerges when information evolves from incomplete (in period 1) to complete (in period 2).

Additionally, the case of a negative tax (an output subsidy) also emerges in both informational contexts when the regulator's environmental conscience is sufficiently low. In these circumstances, the market distortion due to underproduction is much stronger than the distortion due to the environmental damage and, thus, there is a subsidy per unit of output. Furthermore, in the signaling context, the polluter has an incentive to be perceived by the regulator as a low-cost firm (a technically efficient firm), which may lead the low-cost firm to increase its output level of period 1 (direct-signaling effect). The regulator is thus induced in this way to increase the per-unit output subsidy (or per-unit emissions subsidy) with respect to the symmetric information context. In addition, and to reinforce the incentive of the high-cost firm to misrepresent itself as a low-cost firm, the regulator has to make the upward distortions of period 1 output less costly (indirect-signaling effect). This is achieved by increasing the amount of the subsidy in period 1. To conclude, these two effects reinforce each other and lead to the subsidy in the signaling context to be at least not lower than that under symmetric information.

The remainder of the chapter contains five sections. In Section 2 the model is described. Section 3 presents the main results of the analysis when the regulator is worried about pollution. We first determine, as a benchmark, the optimal level of taxes in a symmetric information context. In subsection 3.1 we examine optimal taxation under asymmetric information, and we then compare this tax level with that prevailing in the symmetric information setting; in subsection 3.2 the impact of asymmetric information on welfare is analyzed; in subsection 3.3 the relationship between taxation and pollution damage is considered under symmetric and asymmetric information; finally, subsection 3.4 is devoted to the analysis of these issues when the regulator values the output more than environmental quality. Conclusions are drawn in Section 4.

Chapter 2

THE MODEL

Consider a single industry in which a monopolistic firm produces for two periods, t=1,2. In each period t the inverse demand function for the good produced is linear and given by

$$p_t = 1 - q_t , \tag{1}$$

where p_t denotes the unit price in period t when q_t units of output are sold in such period.

Demand given in (1) can be seen as originating from the maximization problem of a representative consumer with a utility linear in money (or in a numeraire representing the rest of the economy), and quadratic in the product of the industry under consideration. Further, this inverse demand function remains unchanged from one period to the next. Consider also that production of output produces environmental emissions, and in particular, each unit of output corresponds with one unit of emissions, so that $e_t = q_t$.

In addition, assume that the firm causes emissions that damage the environment. Following Ulph (1996), the environmental damage, *ED*, is measured in each period t by the strictly convex function

$$ED_t = \frac{d}{2}(q_t)^2 , \tag{2}$$

where d, $d>0$, is an exogenous parameter indicating the regulator's ecological conscience.

The marginal production cost of the firm determines both its production and emissions levels. Such cost is constant in the output and also across periods. In particular, it adopts either a low or a high value randomly. Specifically,

$$\tilde{c} = \begin{cases} 0, \text{ with probability } \gamma \\ c, \text{ with probability } 1-\gamma \end{cases} \tag{3}$$

where γ, $\gamma \in (0,1)$, is taken as exogenous, and the technological parameter c, $c>0$, represents the bad realization of the marginal cost or, equivalently, the efficiency gap between the high-cost firm (that which produces and pollutes a small amount) and the low-cost one (that which produces and pollutes a larger quantity). Parameter γ denotes the probability that the firm becomes efficient in terms of production costs, while its counterpart $1-\gamma$ stands for the probability corresponding with an inefficient realization of the firm. It is further assumed that both players, the polluting firm and the regulator, are risk-neutral and that the discount factor between periods is one.

Given the inverse demand defined in (1) and the environmental damage function stated in (2), additional restrictions ought to be imposed on parameters c and d, in such a way that they satisfy the following relationship:

ASSUMPTION 1: $0 < c < \dfrac{2}{d+1}$.

This assumption ensures that the firm produces a positive quantity and make positive profits at equilibrium for any realization of production cost, and any type of regulator's beliefs about the nature of the firm.

As indicated, the regulator uses output taxes as a decision variable to control the firm's emissions in each production period. The tax game involves four stages. At the beginning of period 1 (first stage) and before observing the output and emissions choice of the firm for such period, the regulator acts as a Stackelberg leader in setting the environmental tax for period 1, T_1. At this moment, the regulator has less information than the firm (vertical asymmetric information). Given the prior probability assessment concerning the type of the firm and the tax chosen in period 1, in the second stage of the game the firm acts as Stackelberg follower in deciding its period 1 output and emissions level q_1. It is assumed that, at the end of this period, q_1 is observed by the regulator, from which it updates its probability assessment regarding the firm's type. Let $\gamma(q_1)$ be the common updated probability assessment as to the likelihood of the firm producing and polluting a lot.

Next, at the beginning of period 2 and given the updated beliefs after observing the firm's output and emissions of period 1, the regulator announces and commits (in the third stage of the game) to a period 2 per unit output tax, T_2. Finally, in the fourth stage of the game, the firm chooses its profit-maximizing output and emissions of period 2, q_2, given the updated probability assessment $\gamma(q_1)$ and the tax T_2 chosen for such period.

In each period the regulator requires a per-unit charge so as to maximize the expected social welfare per period. This is composed of the un-weighted sum of the consumer surplus, the firm's profit and the governmental revenue from pollution tax minus the environmental damage caused by firm's production. Namely,

$$W_t(q_t) = CS_t(q_t)+\Pi_t(q_t)+R_t(q_t)-ED_t(q_t). \tag{4}$$

The equilibrium concept we use for solving the proposed pollution-tax game is the Bayesian separating equilibrium, in which the output and emissions level of period 1 must constitute a Bayesian equilibrium, while the output and emissions level of period 2 must be chosen optimally given the updated probability assessments, and the beliefs must satisfy the Bayes' rule (when it applies). Hence, while period 1 is characterized by incomplete and asymmetric information, in period 2 complete information is restored.

Chapter 3

RESULTS

Until subsection 3.4 we restrict the analysis to the case in which environmental damage is more valued than the output; namely, values of parameter d are sufficiently high as such $1<d<(2-c)/c$. That is, we address the case of a regulator that is very concerned with environmental quality.

Let's consider first the context in which the information about the firm's type is shared by the regulator, so that both enjoy the same level of information. In such case, the firm's output and emissions in each period t are given by

$$q_t^* = \frac{1-\tilde{c}-T_t}{2}, \ \tilde{c} \in \{0,c\}, \tag{5}$$

where superscript * denotes the symmetric information context. Thus, the regulator faces the problem

$$\max_{T_t} W_t = \frac{3-d}{2}\left(\frac{1-\tilde{c}-T_t}{2}\right)^2 + T_t\frac{1-\tilde{c}-T_t}{2}, \tag{6}$$

in each period t. Solving problem (6) affords the following result.

Lemma 1. Under symmetric information, and whenever $d>1$, the regulator chooses, in each period t, the environmental tax $T_{tL}^* = (d-1)/(d+1)$ for a firm that produces and pollutes a large amount, and $T_{tH}^{*} = (d-1)(1-c)/(d+1)$ for a firm producing and emitting a small quantity.

When selecting the optimal environmental tax in a symmetric information context, the regulator simply takes into account the fact that the firm's output and emissions are the ones that correspond with a (non-strategic) monopoly. Thus, in the trade off between underproduction due to the exercise of market power and the environmental damage caused by the emissions, it sets a positive tax. As it might have been expected, the tax is higher for a (low-cost) firm that pollutes a large quantity than for a (high-cost) firm that pollutes a little. That is, $T_{tL}^{*} > T_{tH}^{*}$, with both increasing with the regulator's ecological conscience, $\partial T_{tk}^{*}/\partial d > 0$, *k*=*L*,*H*. On the other hand, the environmental tax imposed to the firm that pollutes a little, T_{tH}^{*}, decreases as parameter *c* increases, $\partial T_{tH}^{*}/\partial c > 0$, since the level of (production and) emissions of such firm decreases with *c*. Finally, an increase in parameter γ leads to an increase in the expected tax, $T_{t}^{*} = [(d-1)/(d+1)][1-(1-\gamma)c]$, that is, $\partial T_{t}^{*}/\partial \gamma > 0$. This is due to the fact that based on the regulator's prior beliefs about the nature of the firm, a low-cost realization is more likely.

Further, the optimal output and emissions levels for the firm that pollutes a large amount and for that which pollutes a low amount are given by $q_{tL}^{*} = 1/(d+1)$ and $q_{tH}^{*} = (1-c)/(d+1)$, respectively. In turn, the social welfare values associated with the existence of a high- or low-cost polluting firm are, respectively, $W_{tL}^{*} = 1/2(d+1)$ and $W_{tH}^{*} = (1-c)^{2}/2(d+1)$, from which it immediately holds that $W_{tL}^{*} > W_{tH}^{*}$, i.e. a firm that produces and pollutes a large amount (in absolute terms) is socially better than one that produces and pollutes a low amount, despite the regulator's worries about environmental quality.

3.1. The Impact of Asymmetric Information on Taxes

To examine how things evolve in the (more realistic) context of asymmetric information, we assume that the observation of q_1—the period 1 firm's output and emissions level—conveys full information concerning its technological characteristic of a firm that produces and pollutes a large amount or one that produces and pollutes a low amount, by which the game in period 2 becomes a complete information game with the regulator fully informed. In other words, we look for a separating equilibrium.

A separating equilibrium is in this setting a list of players' actions and beliefs, such as $\{T_1^s(\widetilde{c}), q_1^s(\widetilde{c}, T_1^s), \gamma(q_1^s(\cdot)), T_2^*(\widetilde{c}, q_1^s(\cdot)), q_2^*(T_2^*(\cdot), q_1^s(\cdot))\}$ of the following form:

$$T_1^s(\widetilde{c}) = T_1^s \text{, for all } \widetilde{c} \in \{0, c\}, \tag{7}$$

$$q_1^s(\cdot) = \begin{cases} q_{1L}^s, \text{if } \widetilde{c} = 0 \\ q_{1H}^s, \text{if } \widetilde{c} = c \end{cases} \tag{8}$$

$$\gamma(\cdot) = \begin{cases} 1, \text{if } q_1^s = q_{1L}^s \\ 0, \text{if } q_1^s = q_{1H}^s \end{cases} \tag{9}$$

$$T_2^*(\cdot) = \begin{cases} T_{2L}^*, \text{if } q_1^s = q_{1L}^s \\ T_{2H}^*, \text{if } q_1^s = q_{1H}^s \end{cases} \tag{10}$$

and

$$q_2^*(\cdot) = \begin{cases} q_{2L}^*, \text{if } q_1^s = q_{1L}^s \\ q_{2H}^*, \text{if } q_1^s = q_{1H}^s \end{cases} \tag{11}$$

where subscripts H and L denote the firm that pollutes a little and that which pollutes a lot, respectively, and superscripts s and * stand for signaling and complete information contexts, respectively. That is, the regulator selects a period 1 tax, T_1^s, given the probability assessment of the firm being one that produces and pollutes a lot; and the polluting firm chooses a period 1 output and emissions level, q_1^s, given the tax to be paid. Next, for every q_1^s quoted, the regulator forms an updated belief about the type of firm (and the amount of its emissions) and sets T_{2k}^*, k=L,H, the optimal environmental tax for period 2 in a complete information setting, and the polluting firm selects q_{2k}^*, the optimal output and emissions level for such a period. Updated beliefs $\gamma(q_1^s)$ are unrestricted, except that the Bayes' rule is used to form them for actions with positive probability in equilibrium. As usual, a separating equilibrium such as the one defined in (7)-(11) is determined by working backwards from the second period to the first one.

Given that period 2 becomes a complete information period, maximization of the firm's profits in such period yields to the production and emission levels given in (5), and taxes given in Lemma 1. That is,

$$T_2^* = \frac{(d-1)(1-\tilde{c})}{d+1}, \ \tilde{c} \in \{0, c\}, \tag{12}$$

where it can be observed that the higher the regulator's ecological conscience, the higher the tax imposed to the firm, $\partial T_2^* / \partial d > 0$. On the other hand, the lower the firm's marginal cost of production and emissions, the greater the environmental tax. In this case, the regulator places a high value on the environment quality, and the more (output and) pollution emitted, the higher the per-unit output and emissions tax. This, in turn, leads the firm to have an incentive to be perceived as one that produces and pollutes a low amount, in order to bear a lower pollution tax in period 2.[2]

From (5) and (12), the optimal output produced and the pollutant emitted by the monopolist in period 2 is $q_2^* = (1-\tilde{c})/(d+1)$, by which its maximized profit in this period amounts to

$$\Pi_2^* = \left(\frac{1-\tilde{c}}{d+1}\right)^2. \tag{13}$$

Denote by Π_{2L}^* the maximized period 2 profit of the firm that produces and pollutes a lot when it signaled itself as such in period 1, and by $\Pi_{2L}(\gamma(\cdot)=0)$ the maximized profit of such firm when it misrepresented as one that produces and pollutes a little. Similarly, let Π_{2H}^* be the maximized profit of the firm in period 2 when it pollutes a little and signaled itself as such, and $\Pi_{2H}(\gamma(\cdot)=1)$ the firm's maximized profit in period 2 when the

---

[2] The contrary holds when $d<1$, in which case the environmental tax for period 2 becomes negative for each type of firm (a subsidy per unit of pollutant emitted) and higher when the firm produces and pollutes a lot than when it produces and pollutes a lower amount. See subsection 3.4 below.

regulator believes it pollutes a large amount. The following lemma summarizes the incentive of the firm to behave opportunistically.

Lemma 2. Whenever $d>1$, the polluting firm wishes to be perceived as one that (produces and) generates a low amount of emissions.

Proof. See Appendix A.

The lemma states that, regardless of its true technological characteristic, the polluting firm has an incentive to be perceived by the regulator as being one that emits a low amount. This is due to the fact that, if the regulator's valuation of the environmental damage is high enough, it taxes the firm with a lower environmental tax when it believes that the firm generates a low level of pollution.

In period 1, the firm has private information concerning its technology of production and emissions, whereby the environmental tax charged in this period, T_1^s (superscript s stands for signaling), will be the same for both type of firms. Given that T_1^s is announced and committed before the firm produces and pollutes, we need to determine the optimal period 1 output and emissions of the firm for any tax. In a separating equilibrium, the firm signals each of its possible types by selecting a different level of output and emissions in period 1. Thus, it seems reasonable to assume that the output and emissions level q_{1H}^s of a firm producing and emiting a low amount are associated with updated belief $\gamma(q_{1H}^s)=0$ and the output and emissions q_{1L}^s of a firm that produces and emits a large amount with posterior belief $\gamma(q_{1L}^s)=1$. In addition, and to restrict the out-of-equilibrium updated beliefs, it suffices that $\gamma(z_1)=1$ for any other output level z_1 different than q_{1L}^s and q_{1H}^s, a restriction that punishes any deviation from the equilibrium path as much as possible.

Denoting by superscript m the monopoly regime, it is clear that to form part of a separating equilibrium the period 1 output and emissions level of the firm that produces and emits a large amount has to be

$$q_{1L}^s = q_{1L}^m . \tag{14}$$

In addition, the following incentive compatibility conditions

$$\Pi_{1H}^{m} - \Pi_{1H}(q_{1H}^{s}) \leq \Pi_{2H}^{*} - \Pi_{2H}(\gamma(q_{1H}^{m}) = 1), \tag{15}$$

and

$$\Pi_{1L}^{m} - \Pi_{1L}(q_{1H}^{s}) \geq \Pi_{2L}(\gamma(q_{1L}^{m}) = 0) - \Pi_{2L}^{*}, \tag{16}$$

must hold. Succinctly, condition (14) indicates that the best the firm that produces and pollutes a large amount can do in period 1 is to produce the profit-maximizing output and emissions corresponding to a simple monopolist of this type. Inequality (15) is the incentive compatibility condition for a firm that produces and emits a low amount. It states that such a firm would prefer to produce output and emissions q_{1H}^{s} in period 1 (a level that may or may not differ from q_{1H}^{m}, the profit-maximizing output and emissions level as a high-cost monopoly under complete information) and convince the regulator that it is a firm that emits a lower amount, rather than producing and emitting q_{1H}^{m} and then be perceived as one that (produces and) pollutes a lot. Finally, condition (16) is the self-selection constraint for a firm that pollutes a large amount. It establishes that such firm would prefer to produce output q_{1H}^{m} in period 1 and then be perceived as one that pollutes a lot, rather than be understood as one that pollutes less by being forced to produce the output and emissions level q_{1H}^{s} in period 1.

The solution of these conditions enables us to obtain the period 1 outputs and emissions levels that form part of a separating sequential equilibrium. They are summarized in the following lemma.

Lemma 3. When $d>1$, a cut-off value of parameter d exists, $d_1=1+2^{1/2}$, such that the firm's output and emissions in period 1 forming part of a separating sequential equilibrium are as follows:

(i) $q_{1H}^{s} = \frac{1-T_1}{2} - \frac{c}{2} \equiv q_{1H}^{m}$, when the firm is of high-cost and emits a low amount of pollution, and $q_{1L}^{s} = \frac{1-T_1}{2} \equiv q_{1L}^{m}$, when it is of low-cost and emits a large amount, if $d<d_1$ and $c\geq 1-1/d$.

(ii) $q_{1H}^{s}=\frac{1-T_1}{2}-\frac{\sqrt{(d-1)[4+(d-1)c]c}}{2(d+1)}$, when the firm is of high-cost and pollutes a low amount , and $q_{1L}^{s}=\frac{1-T_1}{2}\equiv q_{1L}^{m}$, when it is a low-cost firm and pollutes a large amount, if $d<d_1$ and $c<1-1/d$, or whenever $d\geq d_1$, regardless the value adopted by parameter c.

Proof. See Appendix A.

Part (i) of Lemma 3 states that when the regulator's ecological conscience is moderate and the emissions of the high-cost firm (that emits a low amount) are very different to emissions of the low-cost firm (that emits a large amount), the former needs not to produce and emit less than q_{1H}^{m}, the level as a simple monopolist that produces and pollutes a low amount, to distinguish itself from the latter. In this case, the emissions of the firm that pollutes a little cannot be easily imitated by a firm that pollutes a large amount, and the equilibrium that arises may be called a trivial separating equilibrium (TSE, henceforth). In this case, when taxing the firm the regulator simply considers the trade off between output and emissions as under symmetric information.

Nevertheless, the incentive reflected in Lemma 2 may also lead to the (high-cost) firm that emits a low amount—in order to distinguish itself from the (low-cost) firm that emits a large amount—to reduce its output and emissions of period 1 below the level that would maximize profits as a simple monopolist under complete information; namely, $q_{1H}^{s}<q_{1H}^{m}$. This happens when the regulator's ecological conscience d is moderate and the cost c of the firm that generates a low amount of emissions is sufficiently low, or when d is sufficiently high, irrespective of the value of parameter c, as claimed in Part (ii) of Lemma 3. In this case, the incentive to mislead the regulator is very strong due to gaining in period 2. Thus the (high-cost) firm that pollutes already a low amount is obliged to reduce its production and emissions to a level that a (low-cost) firm that pollutes a large amount finds too costly to imitate. This firm then reacts by simply producing in period 1 the output and emissions that equal the profit-maximizing level, $q_{1L}^{s}=q_{1L}^{m}$. In this case, a signaling effect emerges with respect to the symmetric information context, and it yields a reduction on expected period 1 production and pollution with respect to the existing level, if the firm

behaved as a simple monopolist. This is the so-called non-trivial separating equilibrium (NTSE, onwards).

It is not difficult to show that the greater the environmental conscience (denoting a regulator more concerned about emissions and less about production), the more likely is to find a NTSE. Indeed, whenever $d_1 \geq 1+2^{1/2}$, signaling always leads to a deviation from the output and emissions levels of the (high-cost) firm that produces and pollutes a little under complete information, regardless of the value adopted by the cost parameter c.

Figure 1 below depicts both the TSE and NTSE regions in the $\{d,c\}$-space of parameters, where the continuous line dividing both regions is the locus defined by condition $c=1-1/d$.

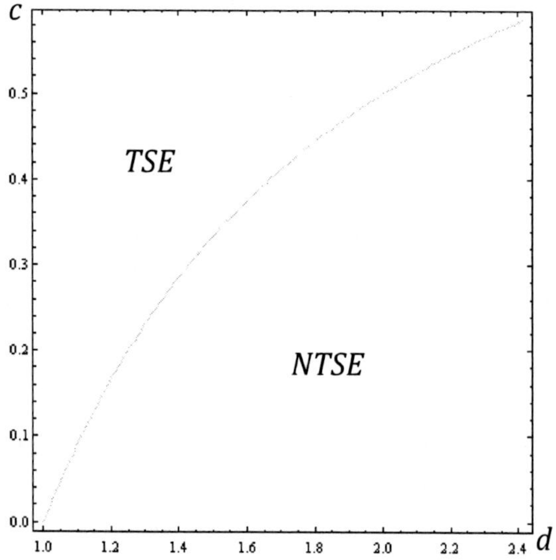

Figure 1. Regions of TSE and NTSE in the {d,c}-space of parameters (1<d<1+21/2).

Now, the regulator takes the unique separating equilibrium stated in Lemma 3 as given and determines the pollution tax that maximizes its objective function in period 1. Such tax is formally given in the following lemma.

Lemma 4. Let $d>1$ and defining the cut-off value $d_1=1+2^{1/2}$. When the firm signals its technology through the output and emissions level of period 1, the optimal pollution tax for such period is as follows:

(i) $T_1^s = \frac{d-1}{d+1}[1-(1-\gamma)c]$, if $d<d_1$ and $c \geq 1-1/d$.

(ii) $T_1^s = \frac{d-1}{d+1}\left[1-(1-\gamma)\frac{\sqrt{(d-1)[4+(d-1)c]c}}{d+1}\right]$, if $d<d_1$ and $c<1-1/d$,

or whenever $d>d_1$, regardless the value of parameter c.

Proof. See Appendix A.

Behind the environmental tax stated in part (i) of Lemma 4 is the consideration of the trade off between environmental damage and output, as occurs under symmetric information (since signaling leads to no deviation of output and emissions of any type of firm with respect to the output and emissions level prevailing under symmetric information). The difference between both informational contexts lies on the fact that, under signaling, T_1^s is the tax paid in period 1 by both type of firms, whereas in the symmetric information case the tax paid in period 1 differs from one type of firm to other, $T_{1L}^* > T_{1H}^*$. So, T_1^s evolves with parameters d, c and γ as T_1^*—the expected tax under symmetric information—does.[3]

In the conditions of part (ii), however, the regulator when setting T_1^s considers the signaling cost suffered by the (high-cost) firm that produces and pollutes a little. In fact, T_1^s increases with parameter d, because this leads the regulator to value higher the environmental damage and to the polluting firm to have a stronger incentive to be perceived as one that produces and pollutes a low amount. This increases in turn the signaling cost of the (high-cost) firm that truly pollutes a low amount, as the regulator increases the tax. However, T_1^s decreases with increments in the cost parameter c, the cost of the firm that pollutes a little amount, because the signaling cost decreases. In particular, when parameter c is high enough for a TSE to prevail, signaling is costless and hence the optimal pollution tax will be the same as under symmetric information (see part (i) of Proposition 1 below). Finally, the size of T_1^s increases with γ, the probability of the firm being one that pollutes a lot, because this makes it less likely that signaling is costly.

---

[3] See Lemma 1.

Turning back to Lemma 3, the firm's output and emissions of period 1 are

$$q_{1H}^{s}=\begin{cases}\dfrac{1-c}{d+1}-\dfrac{\gamma(d-1)c}{2(d+1)}, \text{if } d<d_1 \text{ and } c\geq 1-\dfrac{1}{d}\\ \dfrac{1}{d+1}\\ -\dfrac{(2-\gamma+d\gamma)\sqrt{(d-1)[4+(d-1)c]c}}{2(d+1)^2}, \text{if } d<d_1 \text{ and } c<1-\dfrac{1}{d}\\ \qquad \text{or } d>d_1\end{cases} \quad (17)$$

if the firm produces and emits a low amount, and

$$q_{1L}^{s}=\begin{cases}\dfrac{1}{d+1}+\dfrac{(1-\gamma)(d-1)c}{2(d+1)}, \text{if } d<d_1 \text{ and } c\geq 1-\dfrac{1}{d}\\ \dfrac{1}{d+1}\\ +\dfrac{(1-\gamma)(d-1)\sqrt{(d-1)[4+(d-1)c]c}}{2(d+1)^2}, \text{if } d<d_1 \text{ and } c<1-\dfrac{1}{d}\\ \qquad \text{or } d>d_1\end{cases} \quad (18)$$

if it produces and emits a large amount.

From (17) and (18), it immediately follows that under conditions of part (i) of Lemma 3, the expected output and emission levels in period 1 equal those in which the firm behaves as a simple monopolist.

Taking into account the finding of Lemma 1, we may conclude that whenever the information owned by the firm is shared by the regulator, it pays, in expected terms, the tax $T_1^* = [(d-1)/(d+1)][1-(1-\gamma)c]$ in period 1—a tax that the regulator selects by simply balancing output and the environmental damage caused by the monopolist. Thus, any difference between T_1^s and T_1^* must be entirely attributed to the regulator's activity to mitigate the firm's opportunistic behavior in period 1 due to private information it owns. Formally,

Proposition 1. Let $d>1$. A cut-off value of regulator's ecological conscience exists, $d_1=1+2^{1/2}$, such that:

(i) $T_1^s = T_1^*$, if $d<d_1$ and $c \geq 1-1/d$.

(ii) $T_1^s < T_1^*$, if $d<d_1$ and $c<1-1/d$, or whenever $d>d_1$, regardless the value of parameter c.

Part (i) of the proposition states that when signaling is costless (a TSE emerges), any difference between T_1^s and T_1^* disappears because no deviation in firm's behavior exists with respect to a complete information framework. Part (ii), however, reflects an NTSE in which signaling of the (high-cost) firm that pollutes a little is costly, and in such context the regulator reduces the environmental tax with respect to that imposed under symmetric information in order to decrease such a signaling cost. This allows the regulator to better align its incentives with those of the polluting firm. Stated in a different way, if the environmental tax were increased in the signaling context as compared to the symmetric information setting, the (high-cost) firm that produces and pollutes a low amount would find it more difficult to be perceived as such. Indeed, it would be forced to reduce even further its period 1 output and emissions to distinguish itself from the (low-cost) firm that pollutes a large amount, by which output and emissions in period 1 would be depressed even further from their expected levels. This would be beneficial for the environment, but harmful for the consumer surplus, the firm's profit and the revenue accrued by the regulator. Given that the sum of consumer surplus, the firm's profits and the regulator's income outweigh the environmental damage, the regulator significantly decreases the amount of environmental tax in the signaling context with respect to the symmetric information setting. In other words, in the presence of (costly) signaling, the regulator under-taxes the firm with respect to symmetric information.

The existing under-taxation in the signaling context, $| T_1^s - T_1^* |$, is more pronounced, other things being equal, as parameter d increases, due to the increment of the signaling cost. Likewise, it decreases as parameter c increases, because any increment in the technological efficiency gap reduces the signaling cost. Finally, the under-taxation decreases as parameter γ increases, since the expected level of output and emissions in the signaling context approximate to the existing ones, in expected terms, under symmetric information.

3.2. Asymmetric Information and Welfare

Next, we examine how players' welfare is affected by the fact that the polluting firm signals its technology of production and emissions. Since we have dealt with a separating equilibrium, information in period 2 is complete in both contexts, so it suffices to compare the outcomes achieved in period 1.

Proposition 2. Let *d*>1. Compared to the symmetric information context, the presence of asymmetric information and signaling in the first period of the tax game leads to $CS_1^s > CS_1^*$, $\Pi_1^s > \Pi_1^*$, $R_1^s < R_1^*$, $ED_1^s > ED_1^*$, and $W_1^s < W_1^*$.

Proof. See Appendix A.

Regardless the signaling equilibrium being costless or costly, asymmetric information reduces the expected social welfare, as compared to the symmetric information case. When signaling is costless, welfare is depressed despite the fact that $T_1^s = T_1^*$. This is because T_1^s is equally paid by both types of firms, whereas the tax paid by each type of firm under symmetric information is different, $T_{1H}^* < T_1^s < T_{1L}^*$. This yields $q_{1H}^s < q_{1H}^*$ and $q_{1L}^s > q_{1L}^*$, although the output and emissions under signaling are, in expected terms, equal to those existing under symmetric information, $q_1^s = q_1^*$. However, the fact that $q_{1L}^s > q_{1L}^*$ and $q_{1H}^s < q_{1H}^*$ leads to $CS_1^s > CS_1^*$, $\Pi_1^s > \Pi_1^*$ and $ED_1^s > ED_1^*$. Furthermore, $R_1^s < R_1^*$, given that the regulator gets less revenue from the (low-cost) firm that produces and pollutes a large amount, as compared to the symmetric information context. On the other hand, when signaling is costly, the same production and emissions distortions exist and they are even more pronounced. Thus, the aforementioned argument applies.

3.3. Taxes and Marginal Damage: The Role of Asymmetric Information

We now examine the relationship between environmental taxation and pollution damage in each informational context. Concerning the analysis of optimal environmental taxes, literature generally assumes (a) that firms whose production damages the environment are imperfectly competitive, and (b) that information is complete. In this setting, a number of papers have emphasized two kinds of distortions relative to the efficient optimal production level: the distortion provoked by the environmental damage and that caused by under-production due to imperfect market competition (Barnett 1980, Kennedy 1994). From this trade off between output and environmental emissions, a pollution tax leads firms to decrease the environmental damage, but also to reduce their output even further, aggravating the distortions with respect to the pre-existing taxes. Hence, if the new market distortions cannot be directly corrected, the pollution tax the government prefers tends to be placed below the Pigouvian level, i.e. below the marginal damage caused by pollution (see Simpson 1995, among others).[4] Carlsson (2000) extends the analysis to closed-loop models and shows that the optimal levl of pollution taxes is very sensitive both to the information transmission and the effect of any strategic variable on firms' marginal costs.

In our context, taxes imposed by the regulator are also under-Pigouvian, although asymmetric information tends to approximate their levels to the Pigouvian ones. Formally,

Proposition 3. Let $d>1$ and denote marginal environmental damage by *MD*. The polluting firm is taxed below the marginal damage in any informational context; namely, $T_1^* < MD_1^*$ and $T_1^s < MD_1^s$. However, when signaling is costly, under-taxation is lower than when symmetric information holds, i.e. $UT_1^s \equiv | T_1^s - MD_1^s | < | T_1^* - MD_1^* | \equiv UT_1^*$.

Proof. See Appendix A.

This result indicating that the optimal environmental tax is placed below the marginal damage when information is symmetric parallels other previous findings obtained in similar contexts (Buchanan 1969; Barnet 1980). Furthermore, such under-taxation increases with parameter γ, but decreases as d and c increase. In addition to these results, our model provides two conclusions in the asymmetric information and signaling framework. First,

---

4 The Pigouvian tax, set at marginal environmental damage, is efficient only when the economy is otherwise undistorted.

under-taxation survives in such a context. Second, it is not higher than when information is symmetric. In particular, its amount equals that existing under symmetric information when signaling is costless, and it is lower when signaling is costly. Indeed, (costly) signaling approximates taxes to environmental damage because it leads to a reduction of environmental damage, which is more pronounced than that on taxes. Therefore, a regulatory policy of imposing pollution taxes close to environmental damage may be rationalized in a context in which the regulator lacks information, and signaling activities of polluting firms are costly. This reduction of under-taxation disappears when γ, the probability of the firm becomes a large pollutant, increases.

3.4. A Regulator That Worries More about Production and Less about the Environment

In this section we extend the previous analysis to the case in which the regulator's valuation of the environmental damage, *d*, is sufficiently low as $0<d<1$. In a sense, the regulator now values the output more than environmental quality. In this case, a negative tax (subsidy) emerges under complete information, as it can be directly observed from Lemma 1. Furthermore, the per-unit output subsidy is higher for a (low-cost) firm that produces and pollutes a lot than for one that produces and pollutes a lower amount; namely, $S^*_{tL} > S^*_{tH}$, where *S* denotes subsidy. This clearly leads to a revision of the result presented in Lemma 2: the polluting firm is now strongly interested in being perceived as one that produces and pollutes a large amount (the so-called low-cost firm), as a means to increase the amount of the subsidy granted in period 2, and thus, its profits.

Under these circumstances, the conditions needed for a separating equilibrium to exist are now given by

$$q^s_{1H} = q^m_{1H}, \tag{19}$$

$$\Pi^m_{1L} - \Pi_{1L}(q^s_{1L}) \leq \Pi^*_{2L} - \Pi_{2L}(\gamma(q^m_{1L}) = 0), \tag{20}$$

and

$$\Pi^m_{1L} - \Pi_{1H}(q^s_{1L}) \geq \Pi_{2H}(\gamma(q_{1L}) = 1) - \Pi^*_{2H}, \tag{21}$$

where condition (19) indicates the best the (high-cost) firm that produces and pollutes a low amount can do is to simply replicate the profit-maximizing output and emissions of a simple high-cost monopolist under complete information. Conditions (20) and (21) are, respectively, the incentive compatibility constraints for the firm that produces a lot and the one that produces a low amount.

Solving these conditions enables us to obtain the period 1 outputs and emissions that form part of a separating equilibrium.

Lemma 5. When $0<d<1$, the output and emissions of period 1 that form part of a separating equilibrium are:

(i) $q_{1L}^{s} = \frac{1-T_1}{2} \equiv q_{1L}^{m}$, if the (low-cost) firm produces and pollutes a large quantity, and $q_{1H}^{s} = \frac{1-c-T_1}{2} \equiv q_{1H}^{m}$, if it produces and pollutes a low quantity, whenever parameters c and d satisfy $c \geq 1-d$.

(ii) $q_{1L}^{s} = \frac{1-c-T_1}{2} + \frac{\sqrt{(1-d)[4-(3+d)c]c}}{2(1+d)}$, if the firm is one that produces and pollutes a large quantity, and $q_{1H}^{s} = \frac{1-c-T_1}{2} \equiv q_{1H}^{m}$, if it is a firm that produces and pollutes a low quantity, whenever parameters c and d satisfy $c<1-d$.

Proof. See Appendix A.

In this case, the best that the firm generating a low emissions level can do is to simply choose the monopolistic level of output and emissions corresponding to its type, $q_{1H}^{s} = (1-c-T_1)/2 \equiv q_{1H}^{m}$. The (low-cost) firm that produces and pollutes a large amount may set, however, the levels according to its type, $q_{1L}^{s} = (1-T_1)/2 \equiv q_{1L}^{m}$, when parameters c and d satisfy $c \geq 1-d$ or higher levels than those corresponding to its true type, $q_{1L}^{s} = \frac{1-c-T_1}{2} + \frac{\sqrt{(1-d)[4-(3+d)c]c}}{2(1+d)} > q_{1L}^{m}$, when $c<1-d$. We refer to the first case as a TSE, and the second one as an NTSE. Figure 2 below depicts the region of parameters where each equilibrium holds.

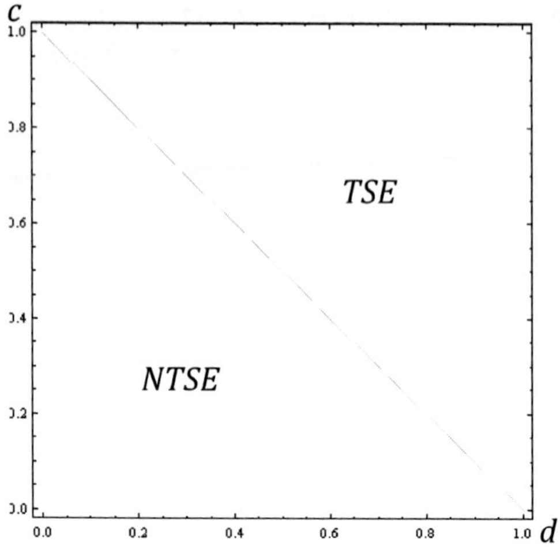

Figure 2. Regions of TSE and NTSE in the $\{d,c\}$-space of parameters ($0<d<1$)

Next, we are able to determine the optimal tax in period 1 for both types of realizations of the firm.

Lemma 6. When $0<d<1$ and the firm signals its technology of production and emissions, the optimal tax for period 1 is (negative) a subsidy per unit of pollutant emitted, S_1^s, given by:

(i) $S_1^s = \frac{d-1}{1+d}[c-1-\gamma c]$, if $c \geq 1-d$.

(ii) $S_1^s = \frac{d-1}{1+d}\left[c-1-\frac{\gamma\sqrt{(1-d)[4-(3+d)c]c}}{1+d}\right]$, if $c<1-d$.

Proof. See Appendix A.

As mentioned, the amount of subsidy in this context depends on the importance of the output distortion due to market power in the light of the environmental damage (signaling effect), which leads the (low-cost) firm that produces a large amount to produce at least not below the period 1 monopolistic optimal level. The size of the subsidy decreases as parameter d increases, because the relative value of production versus environmental damage also decreases, and the incentive of the firm to be perceived as one that produces and pollutes a large amount is reduced. The subsidy also decreases with respect to *c*, the technological gap between both types of firm, because it reduces both the output and the firm's incentive to be perceived as one that produces a large quantity. Finally, the subsidy increases with the probability of the firm producing a large quantity, since this prior belief increases the expected output and the amount of the signaling effect.

The (low-cost) firm that truly produces and pollutes a large amount may be forced to produce and pollute a level not lower than that corresponding to the monopolistic equilibrium. This has a negative impact on the environmental quality but it increases output. So, when the firm that pollutes a large amount needs to produce and pollute, to signal its true type, more than the amount corresponding to its type as a monopolist, the regulator increases the amount of subsidy granted in period 1 to exacerbate the increase in output. Formally, when comparing the size of the subsidies granted in each informational context, the following holds.

Proposition 4. When $0<d<1$, then:

(i) $S_1^s = S_1^*$, if $c \geq 1-d$.

(ii) $S_1^s > S_1^*$, if $c<1-d$.

Part (i) of Proposition 4 refers to the case in which signaling to convey information to the regulator is costless. Then the subsidy equals its expected level under symmetric information. In part (ii), however, signaling is costly and leads to an increase in expected output and emissions. Since the regulator is worried about the output level, it wishes to exacerbate the signaling cost by increasing the subsidy granted. This reinforces the incentive of the (high-cost) firm that produces a lower quantity to be perceived as one that produces a large amount and, thus, the firm that produces a large quantity is obliged to increase its production further.

Finally, the welfare implications of asymmetric information and signaling follows straightforwardly from the fact that output and emissions levels of the polluting firm are

$$q_{1L}^{s} = \begin{cases} \dfrac{1}{1+d} - \dfrac{(1-\gamma)(1-d)c}{2(1+d)}, \text{if } c \geq 1-d \\ \dfrac{1-c}{1+d} + \dfrac{(1+d+\gamma-d\gamma)\sqrt{(1-d)[4-(3+d)c]c}}{2(1+d)^2}, \text{if } c < 1-d \end{cases} \quad (22)$$

when it produces and pollutes a large amount, and

$$q_{1H}^{s} = \begin{cases} \dfrac{1-c}{1+d} + \dfrac{\gamma(1-d)c}{2(1+d)}, \text{if } c \geq 1-d \\ \dfrac{1-c}{1+d} + \dfrac{\gamma(1-d)\sqrt{(1-d)[4-(3+d)c]c}}{2(1+d)^2}, \text{if } c < 1-d \end{cases} \quad (23)$$

when the firm produces and pollutes a small amount. Thus, taken into account that, under symmetric information, $q_{1L}^{*} = 1/(1+d)$ and $q_{1H}^{*} = (1-c)/(1+d)$, we conclude that, whenever signaling is costless, the (low-cost) firm that produces more, reduces its production and emissions as compared with symmetric information context, $q_{1L}^{s} < q_{1L}^{*}$, due to the fact that $S_1^s < S_{1L}^{*}$, whereas the (high-cost) firm that produces a low quantity increases theirs, $q_{1H}^{s} > q_{1H}^{*}$, since $S_1^s > S_{1H}^{*}$. Overall, this leads the expected output to be lower than that under symmetric information, $q_1^s < q_1^*$. So, $CS_1^s < CS_1^*$, $\Pi_1^s < \Pi_1^*$, $ED_1^s < ED_1^*$, and $W_1^s < W_1^*$. On the other hand, in the case in which signaling is costly for the (low-cost) firm that produces a large output, it follows that $q_1^s > q_1^*$, which leads to the opposite set of results than those aforementioned.

Chapter 4

CONCLUDING REMARKS

The analysis of pollution taxes and charges is relevant not only from a theoretical perspective, but also for political discussion and practical implications. Policymakers need to understand how such instruments work when considering whether or not they should be introduced in the future and to what extent. The main purpose of this research has been to examine the optimal pollution tax/subsidy policy in a monopolistic industry in which the firm's technology of production and emissions is unobservable for the regulator, and it can be inferred after observing a firm's signal. An extensive literature review has revealed the lack of research into models of optimal environmental taxation considering the problem of asymmetric information—in our case, vertical asymmetric information and signaling—in the presence of heterogeneous firms. Furthermore, the dynamic analysis here presented is enriched by considering a wide range of values for the regulator's environmental conscience. As observed, the assumption that firms have private information and can transmit it by their output and emissions behavior complicates the taxation issue, since the regulator must consider the signaling effect when the tax to be paid by the firm is chosen. However, the assumption that firms have private information that the regulator can only infer allows for a closer approximation to real-life situations.

In this context, a number of scenarios have been examined in this chapter depending upon the level of production and emissions costs of the firm and the value the regulator attaches to environmental degradation. The results shown above indicate that whenever the regulator places a high value on environmental damage, the (first period) environmental tax in the case in which the monopolist signals its production and emissions costs through the output and emissions produced in such period is not higher than that when the firm does not need to signal such costs, because information is symmetric. If the regulator's ecological conscience is sufficiently high, the incentive of the monopolist to be perceived as a firm that pollutes a low amount leads it to under-produce and under-emit in the first (asymmetric information) period when the gap of technical efficiency is low enough, or simply to produce and emit in the first period the level that corresponds to symmetric information, when the gap is sufficiently high. Thus, in order to make it easier for the (high-cost) firm that pollutes a low amount to be perceived as such, the regulator is obliged to reduce the environmental tax in the (first period) asymmetric information context with respect to the level prevailing under symmetric information. In sum, the regulator charges, in the asymmetric information period, a pollution tax lower or equal than that it would charge in the symmetric information context.

On the other hand, when the regulator's valuation of the environmental damage is so low that consumption outweighs environmental damage, the pollution tax becomes negative (a subsidy per unit of output) in both informational contexts, and its size in the signaling case is greater than or equal to that prevailing in the symmetric information scenario.

Overall, these findings suggest that a regulator may adjust the imposed taxes/ subsidies according to the existing informational context. In the case when signaling is costly, and the regulator has a high environmental conscience, there is a time-increasing path in pollution taxes, so that the regulator increases taxes after observing the first period output and emissions. Similarly, when the regulator's environmental conscience is low, a time-decreasing path in subsidies is found, so that after observing the first-period output and emissions, the regulator decreases subsidies to equalize them with those of symmetric information. To conclude, the symmetric information conditions restored in the second period reduce the initial existing gap between taxes and subsidies obtained from different environmental consciences. As it is well known, much literature on environmental economics has suggested the importance of environmental values on environmental policies. Our theoretical findings back up such assessment, although they also remark the importance of informational conditions in taxation schemes. In turn, the obtained results emphasized that holding environmental values constant across periods, optimal taxation may considerably vary depending on the informational conditions that prevail in each period.

These results open up a number of avenues for further research. For example, the model could be adapted to analyze the strategic behavior of firms in the context of environmental tax/subsidy choice at the international level. In particular, it may be used to forecast the strategic behavior of firms when regulators pursue to maximize social welfare by maximizing output. The analysis of such strategic behavior may allow us to understand the long-term environmental consequences of output incentives provided by the current anti-crises policies. Furthermore, our model could be adapted to include investment decisions to abate and the trade offs between abatement and tax payment under asymmetric information and signaling. Other refinements extending the current set up to multiple polluting firms and ecological conscience on the part of consumers may also be considered. These and other similar suggestions are left for future research.

ACKNOWLEDGMENT

The authors would like to thank, without implicating, Juan-Pablo Montero and other participants in the Atlantic Meeting held in A Toxa (Galicia, Spain) for helpful comments and suggestions that improved the content of this chapter. Both authors gratefully acknowledge financial aid form the Galician Regional Government (Xunta de Galicia) through Grants INCITE09201042PR (Antelo) and ECO2009-14586-CO2-02 (Loureiro). Manel Antelo and Maria L. Loureiro are Associate Professors of the Department of Economic Analysis, University of Santiago de Compostela, Spain.

APPENDIX A

Proof of Lemma 2. If the firm emits a large amount of pollution but it has signalled itself as a firm that emits a small amount, and, consequently, it must pay in period 2 the tax designed for such a firm, then its maximized profit in period 2 is

$$\Pi_{2L}(\gamma(\cdot)=0)=\left(\frac{2+(d-1)c}{2(d+1)}\right)^2=\left(q_{2L}+\frac{(d-1)c}{2(d+1)}\right)^2 \tag{A1}$$

and it can be easily checked that (A1) is greater than Π^*_{2L}, the maximized profit of the low-cost firm under complete information.

Similarly, if the firm emits a low amount of pollution, but the regulator believes that it potentially emits a large amount, then its maximized profit in period 2 is given by

$$\Pi_{2H}(\gamma(\cdot)=1)=\left(\frac{2-(d-1)c}{2(d+1)}\right)^2=\left(q_{2L}-\frac{(d-1)c}{2(d+1)}\right)^2, \tag{A2}$$

which is greater than Π^*_{2H}. This completes the result claimed in the lemma.

□

Proof of Lemma 3. Particularizing the incentive compatibility conditions defined in (14)-(16), we have, respectively,

$$q_{1L}^{s} = \frac{1-T_1}{2} \equiv q_{1L}^{m}, \tag{A3}$$

$$(1-c-T_1-q_{1H}^{s})q_{1H}^{s} + \left(\frac{1-c}{d+1}\right)^2 \geq \left(\frac{1-c-T_1}{2}\right)^2 + \left(\frac{2-(d-1)c}{2(d+1)}\right)^2, \tag{A4}$$

and

$$\left(\frac{1-T_1}{2}\right)^2 + \left(\frac{1}{d+1}\right)^2 \geq (1-T_1-q_{1H}^{s})q_{1H}^{s} + \left(\frac{2+(d-1)c}{2(d+1)}\right)^2. \tag{A5}$$

By taking condition (A4) as equality, the resulting second-degree equation has

$$q_{1H}^{s} = \frac{1-c-T_1}{2} \pm \frac{\sqrt{(d-1)[4-(d+3)c]c}}{2(d+1)}, \tag{A4a}$$

as roots, while the second-degree equation formed by taking condition (A5) as equality has the following roots

$$q_{1H}^{s} = \frac{1-T_1}{2} \pm \frac{\sqrt{(d-1)[4+(d-1)c]c}}{2(d+1)}. \tag{A5a}$$

Denote by r^- the lowest root of the two obtained in (A4a) and by s^- the lowest root of the two defined in (A5a). Given that $r^- < s^-$, the continuum of separating equilibria is formed by the interval of outputs given by $q_{1H}^{s} \in [r^-, s^-]$. On the other hand, any period 1 output and emissions level strictly less than s^- is a dominated-output and emissions for the firm that produces and emits a little and thereby the separating equilibrium of minimum cost involves the output and emissions $q_{1H}^{s} = s^-$. From here, it is easy to check that $q_{1H}^{s} = (1-c-T_1)/2 < s^-$, when parameters d and c verify $c<1-1/d$. Thus, the period 1 outputs that form part of the (non-trivial) separating equilibrium are $q_{1H}^{s} = s^-$ and $q_{1L}^{s} = q_{1L}^{m}$, which refers to part (ii) of the lemma. Part (i) refers to the case in which $q_{1H}^{s} > s^-$. This occurs when parameters d and c verify condition $c \geq 1-1/d$. In this case, the firm's productions and emissions as a simple monopolist, q_{1H}^{m} if it is of high-cost and q_{1L}^{m} if it is of low-cost, constitute a TSE. Finally, comparison of the threshold value $1-1/d$ with upper-bound $2/(d+1)$ imposed by Assumption 1 allows us to conclude that either a TSE or a NTSE are feasible if $1-1/d < 2/(d+1)$, i.e. if $d < 1+2^{1/2} \equiv d_1$. If, otherwise, $d > 1+2^{1/2} \equiv d_1$, then Assumption 1 implies that $c < 1-1/d$ always holds and thus a NTSE always emerges, irrespective of the value adopted by parameter c. This completes the proof of the lemma. □

Proof of Lemma 4. Given the objective function of the regulator defined in (4), the problem

$$\max_{T_1} W_1 = \frac{3-d}{2}[\gamma(q_{1L}^{s})^2 + (1-\gamma)(q_{1H}^{s})^2] + T_1[\gamma q_{1L}^{s} + (1-\gamma)q_{1H}^{s}], \tag{A6}$$

where q_{1L}^{s} and q_{1H}^{s} are equilibrium outputs and emissions defined in Lemma 3, has

$$0 = \frac{\partial W_1}{\partial T_1} = (3-d)\left[\gamma q_{1L}^{s}\frac{\partial q_{1L}^{s}}{\partial T_1} + (1-\gamma)q_{1H}^{s}\frac{\partial q_{1H}^{s}}{\partial T_1}\right] + \gamma\left(q_{1L}^{s} + T_1\frac{\partial q_{1L}^{s}}{\partial T_1}\right)$$
$$+ (1-\gamma)\left(q_{1H}^{s} + T_1\frac{\partial q_{1H}^{s}}{\partial T_1}\right) \tag{A7}$$

as first-order condition. Finally, solving (A7) yields the result claimed in the lemma. □

Proof of Proposition 2. From (17) and (18), the expected output and emissions of period 1 under costless signaling (TSE) are given by $q_1^{s} = \gamma q_{1L}^{s} + (1-\gamma)q_{1H}^{s} = 1/(d+1) - (1-\gamma)c/(d+1)$, which equal q_1^{*}, the expected output and emissions level under symmetric information. On the other hand, it can be easily shown that $CS_1^{*} = A/2(d+1)^2$, $\Pi_1^{*} = A/(d+1)^2$, $R_1^{*} = A(d-1)/(d+1)^2$, $ED_1^{*} = Ad/2(d+1)^2$, and $W_1^{*} = A/2(d+1)$, where $A=1-(1-\gamma)(2-c)c$. Hence, some algebraic manipulation yields

$$CS_1^s = CS_1^* + \gamma(1-\gamma)\frac{(d-1)(d+3)c^2}{8(d+1)^2}, \tag{A8}$$

$$\Pi_1^s = \Pi_1^* + \gamma(1-\gamma)\frac{(d-1)(d+3)c^2}{4(d+1)^2}, \tag{A9}$$

$$R_1^s = R_1^* - \gamma(1-\gamma)\frac{(d-1)c^2}{(d+1)^2}, \tag{A10}$$

and

$$ED_1^s = ED_1^* + \gamma(1-\gamma)\frac{d(d-1)(d+3)c^2}{8(d+1)^2} \tag{A11}$$

Finally,

$$W_1^s = W_1^* - \gamma(1-\gamma)\frac{(d-1)^2c^2}{d+1}. \tag{A12}$$

On the other hand, if signaling is costly (NTSE), the expected output and emissions are given by

$$q_1^s = \frac{1}{d+1} - (1-\gamma)\frac{\sqrt{(d-1)[4+(d-1)c]c}}{(d+1)^2}, \tag{A13}$$

whereby

$$q_1^s - q_1^* = (1-\gamma)\frac{(d+1)c - \sqrt{(d-1)[4+(d-1)c]c}}{(d+1)^2}, \tag{A14}$$

and the result follows from the fact that $c<1-1/d$. More precisely,

$$q_{1L}^s - q_{1L}^* = (1-\gamma)(d-1)\frac{\sqrt{(d-1)[4+(d-1)c]c}}{2(d+1)^2} > 0, \tag{A15}$$

and

$$q_{1H}^{s}-q_{1H}^{*}=\frac{2(d+1)c-[2+(d-1)\gamma]\sqrt{(d-1)[4+(d-1)c]c}}{2(d+1)^{2}}<0\,, \qquad \text{(A16)}$$

because $2<2+(d-1)\gamma$ and $(d+1)c<[(d-1)(4+(d-1)c)c]^{1/2}$. Hence, $CS_1^s > CS_1^*$, $\Pi_1^s > \Pi_1^*$, $R_1^s < R_1^*$, and $ED_1^s < ED_1^*$. Overall, $W_1^s < W_1^*$. This completes the proof of the proposition. □

Proof of Proposition 3. In the symmetric information context, the marginal environmental damage in period 1 amounts to

$$MD_1^* = \frac{d}{d+1}[1-(1-\gamma)c]\,, \qquad \text{(A17)}$$

and under-taxation to

$$UT_1^* \equiv MD_1^* - T_1^* = \frac{1}{d+1}[1-(1-\gamma)c]\,, \qquad \text{(A18)}$$

which is positive because $(1-\gamma)c<1$. Similarly, in conditions where signaling is costless it follows that $MD_1^s = MD_1^*$ and $T_1^s = T_1^*$, so the amount of under-taxation is the same than that stated in (A18). On the other hand, in the NTSE we must compare T_1^s and

$$MD_1^s = \frac{d}{d+1}\left[1-\frac{(1-\gamma)\sqrt{(d-1)[4+(d-1)c]c}}{d+1}\right]. \qquad \text{(A19)}$$

This affords

$$UT_1^s \equiv MD_1^s - T_1^s = \frac{1}{d+1}\left[1-\frac{(1-\gamma)\sqrt{(d-1)[4+(d-1)c]c}}{d+1}\right], \qquad \text{(A20)}$$

which is positive since $(d-1)^{1/2}[(4+(d-1)c)c]^{1/2}<d+1$ by Assumption 1. Finally, by comparing (A18) and (A20) it follows that

$$UT_1^* - UT_1^s = (1-\gamma)\left[\frac{\sqrt{(d-1)[4+(d-1)c]c}}{d+1} - c\right], \tag{A21}$$

which is strictly positive whenever the signaling is costly. Thus $UT_1^s < UT_1^*$.

□

Proof of Lemma 5. Once the incentive compatibility conditions (20)-(21) are particularized, they become

$$\left(\frac{1-T_1}{2}\right)^2 - (1-T_1-q_{1L}^s)q_{1L}^s \leq \left(\frac{1}{1+d}\right)^2 - \left(\frac{2-(1-d)c}{2(1+d)}\right)^2, \tag{A22}$$

for the (low-cost) firm that produces and emits a large amount, and

$$\left(\frac{1-c-T_1}{2}\right)^2 - (1-c-T_1-q_{1L}^s)q_{1L}^s \geq \left(\frac{2+(1-d)c}{2(1+d)}\right)^2 - \left(\frac{1-c}{1+d}\right)^2, \tag{A23}$$

for the (high-cost) firm that produces and emits a little. When condition (A22) is solved as equality, it yields the roots

$$q_{1L}^s = \frac{1-T_1}{2} \pm \frac{\sqrt{(1-d)[4-(1-d)c]c}}{2(1+d)}. \tag{A22a}$$

Similarly, condition (A23) affords the following roots

$$q_{1L}^s = \frac{1-c-T_1}{2} \pm \frac{\sqrt{(1-d)[4-(3+d)c]c}}{2(1+d)}. \tag{A23a}$$

Denote by v^+ the highest root of the two defined in (A22a) and by u^+ the highest root of the two defined in (A23a). Given that $v^+ > u^+$, the interval of outputs and emissions given by $q_{1L}^s \in [u^+, v^+]$ is non-degenerated and defines the continuum of separating equilibria. The separating equilibrium of minimum cost is then given by $q_{1L}^s = u^+$. Finally, it holds that $u^+ \leq (1-T_1)/2 \equiv q_{1L}^m$ when parameters d and c satisfy $c \geq 1-d$, in which case a

TSE emerges, while $u^{+} > (1-T_1)/2 \equiv q_{1L}^{m}$ when $c<1-d$. In this case there is a NTSE. □

Proof of Lemma 6. By solving the first-order condition $\partial W_1^s / \partial T_1 = 0$ once welfare is evaluated at productions and emissions levels given in part (i) of Lemma 5. Part (ii) is proved as part (i) but with productions and emissions levels given in part (ii) of Lemma 5. □

REFERENCES

Antelo, M. & Loureiro, M.L. (2009). Asymmetric information, signaling and environmental taxes in oligopoly, *Ecological Economics, 68*, 1430-1440.

Barnett, A.H. (1980). The pigouvian tax rule under monopoly, *American Economic Review, 70*, 1037-1041.

Baron, D., Besanko, D. (1985). Regulation, asymmetric information, and auditing, *Rand Journal of Economics*, *15*, 447-470.

Baron, D., Myerson, R.B. (1982). Regulating a monopolist with unknown cost, *Econometrica, 50*, 911-930.

Baumol, W.J. & Oates, W.E. (1988). *The Theory of Environmental Policy*, Cambridge: Cambridge University Press.

Benchekroun, H. & Van Long, N. (1998). Efficiency inducing taxation for polluting oligopolists, *Journal of Public Economics, 70*, 325-342.

Bovenberg, L. (1999). Green tax reforms and the double dividend: an updated reader's guide, *International Tax and Public Finance, 6*, 421-443.

Buchanan, J.M. (1969). External diseconomies, corrective taxes, and market structures, *American Economic Review, 59*, 174-77.

Cairncros, F. (1995). *Green, Inc.*, London: Earthscan Publications Ltd.

Carlsson, F. (2000). Environmental taxation and strategic commitment in duopoly models, *Environmental and Resource Economics, 15*, 243-256.

European Commission (1998). Database on Environmental Taxes in the EU Member States, plus Norway and Switzerland. Evaluation of Environmental Effects of Environmental Taxes, Luxembourg: Office for Official Publications of the European Communities.

Helfand, G. (1999). Standards versus taxes in pollution control. In J.C.J.M. van den Bergh (ed.), *Handbook of Environmental and Resource Economics*, Edward Elgard.

Jung, C., Krutilla, K. & Boyd, R. (1996). Incentives for advanced pollution abatement technology at the industry level: An evaluation of policy alternatives, *Journal of Environmental Economics and Management, 30*,139-148.

Kennedy, P. (1994). Equilibrium pollution taxes in open economies with imperfect competition, *Journal of Environmental Economics and Management, 27*, 49-63.

Lange, A. (2006). The impact of equity-preferences on the stability of international environmental agreements, *Environmental and Resource Economics, 34*, 247-267.

Milliman, S.R. & Prince, R. (1989). Firm incentives to promote technological change in pollution control, *Journal of Environmental Economics and Management, 10*, 248-269.

Morgenstern, R. (1996). Environmental taxes: Dead or alive? Discussion Paper 96-03, Resources for the Future. Washington, DC.

Organization for Economic and Co-operation Development (OECD) (2006). *The Political Economy of Environmentally Related Taxes*, Paris.

Pigou, A. (1920). *The Economics of Welfare*, London: Weindenfeld & Nicholson.

Simpson, R.D. (1995). Optimal pollution taxation in a Cournot duopoly, *Environmental and Resource Economics, 6*, 359-369.

Spulber, D.F. (1985). Effluent regulation and long-run optimality, *Journal of Environmental Economics and Management, 12*, 103-116.

Schöb, R. (2003). The double dividend hypothesis of environmental taxes: A survey, Faculty of Economics and Management, W.P. No. 4, Otto-von-Guericke-University of Magdeburg.

Ulph, A. (1996). Environmental policy and international trade when governments and producers act strategically, *Journal of Environmental Economics and Management, 30*, 265-281.

INDEX